The Bible Told Us:

Prideful Leaders Are Humbled by God

Humble Leaders Are Honored by God

Poetry inspired by Biblical scripture

Esther A. Coleman-Spells

ISBN: 978-0-578-83982-0

DEDICATIONS

Dedicated to my parents, Joseph and Mary Coleman, who taught us God is the Captain of our team

Dedicated to my cousin, Krystle Brooks, who demonstrated how to follow an author's dream

Dedicated to my friends, Martisha and Anjanette, who motivated me to write

Dedicated to my children, Javaughn and Jailyn, for whom I want to fight the good fight

Dedicated to the readers, God's beloved, may your hearts be stirred

There is nothing more precious than to hold in your hearts God's life-changing Word

CONTENTS

PART I

PART II

A Message from the Author

Dear readers,

It is so important to be reminded of the lessons God has repeatedly taught us through the prideful foolishness of others and more specifically, through the pridefulness of leaders in the Bible. Pridefulness is a haughty spirit of arrogance and superiority for which God humbled many prideful leaders through corrective discipline. Those who refused to humble themselves often paid the price with their lives in one way or another. We can avoid being disciplined by God and instead, we can enjoy the faithfulness of God by not repeating their mistakes.

I hope you enjoy reading about some of these life lessons from the Bible presented in the form of poetry. I believe God has inspired and enabled me to present this timeless message of pride before destruction in this particular genre to reach readers across various levels of leadership, readers in different walks of life, and readers of different age groups.

I pray that each of you will be ministered to not only in the area of refraining from pride and arrogance, but also in embracing humility for everyday living and leadership. In each passage, we learn of both the dangers of pride as well as the power of humility. I pray that each of us will desire to grow in Godly love for one another as well as love and reverence for the one and only true, Almighty God.

God Bless You,

Esther Spells

Part I:

Prideful Leaders Are Humbled by God

Humble Leaders Are Honored by God

Based on the Biblical book of Daniel:
Chapters 1-6

Pride goes before destruction,
a haughty spirit before a fall.
Proverbs 16:18 (NIV)

KING NEBUCHADNEZZAR TAKES DANIEL TO BABYLON

Judah was taken by the Babylonian king
It was all in God's plan
God allowed these four young men
To be taken to a foreign land
They remained forever faithful to God
For they knew He was never far
One young man named Daniel,
The king named Belteshazzar

You can have whatever you want
As long as you learn the Babylonian way
They learned the language and the culture
But hid God in their hearts all day
Daniel and his friends, they honored God
One way was through their diet
When it came to what they put in their bodies
They simply refused to stay quiet
The young men were offered the best food and wine
They were told they must be healthy and strong
Give us water and vegetables only they responded
To honor God you can't go wrong
If the guards agree to this restrictive diet and it fails
The guards the king would detest
The guards were afraid that these Jewish teens
Wouldn't stand to compete with the rest

However, the four young men impressed the king
With their strength and ease to learn

Also, Daniel could tell visions and dreams
What a high respect he earned
The king tested these four young men
Found them smart and wise
Placed them in the king's royal service
Only the beginning of their rise

Food for Thought, Heart, and Spirit:

- God can produce positive outcomes even from negative situations.
- God wants His people to have strong faith and strong determination - "No matter what, I will serve the Lord my God" determination.
- If we are faithful to God, He will be faithful to us.
- Trust God - Simple is often sufficient.

KING NEBUCHADNEZZAR'S DREAM OF A STATUE

Nebuchadnezzar was extremely upset
He had a disturbing dream
The king could not interpret an understanding
He called his counseling team
They asked him to tell the dream
They would explain to him what it means
The king said no, I want an explanation
After you tell me the dream
The advisors were confused and said to the king
No one can do what you ask
The king was furious and said to them
Then death to you all is the task
The commander of the king's guard went out
To get started as the king was stewing
But Danial stayed calm and respectfully asked
The why of what they were doing
The commander told him and Daniel asked
If he could speak to the king
Daniel, trusting God, told Nebuchadnezzar
That he could explain the thing
Daniel went home to his loyal friends
They prayed for a heaven-sent answer
Sure enough, their God of Heaven
Showed up and swiftly delivered

Daniel went back to the troubled king
To explain his curious dream

It's not me but God in heaven
Who's revealed what your dream means
You saw an enormous statue
The head was made of pure gold
The chest and arms of silver
This is what God has told
Bronze made up the belly and thighs
Iron made up the legs
More iron and baked clay made up the feet
That's what God has said
Then a stone suddenly appeared
And hit the statue at its feet
The statue fell and crumbled
Like the husks of grain and wheat
The wind swept away the pieces
Did not leave a trace
Then the stone grew until huge
And took up all the space

Dear king, I have told you
What you indeed did dream
Now even more importantly
I'll tell you what this dream means
God has given you power
Over this dominion and of the fold
You, O king, are the statue's head
Made of the purest gold
Silver and bronze, they represent
Inferior kingdoms to arise
They will appear later
After your own kingdom's demise
Yet later another kingdom will come

But just like the iron and clay
They can't bond together
So they'll also fall away
While these unsuitable kingdoms fail
The head of each one a man
God will build another kingdom
That will forever stand
This is the interpretation
Of the dream God gave to you
Trust what I've explained
For every part of it is true

The king fell down to the floor
He thanked Daniel for everything
Your God is the God of all gods
Your God is the Lord of all the Kings
Daniel was lavished with elegant gifts
He was placed in a high position
Remember his friends who also prayed
They were also given recognition
Daniel was promoted to leader
Placed in charge of all the other wise men
And Shadrach, Meshach, and Abednego
Became Babylon's newest admin

Food for Thought, Heart, and Spirit:

- God knows how to get the attention of everyone and anyone, even a powerful king.
- The world cannot impart to us the things we are to understand from God.

- You cannot buy God. You cannot buy wisdom. You cannot buy peace.
- Scared people threaten others.
- Ask God for help to speak with wisdom and tact even when feeling threatened.
- Ask God for the ability to see when others are hurting or afraid. Ask God for the ability to help in some way to God's glory.
- Give thanks to God when he sees fit to use us for His work. It is an honor and a privilege.
- God is always in control.
- God is never unaware.
- God's people intervene for others.
- God is our source for all unanswered questions.
- Remain humble when God uses you to fulfil His purpose.

PROMOTED THROUGH FAITH AND FIRE

The prideful king made an image
The image was made of gold
Everyone must worship this image
The word from the king was told
All of the important people
Gathered around for its dedication
With expectations of everyone
To worship from all the nations
One was supposed to sound
The horn, flute, harp, and lyre
At the sound, worship this image
Or you'll be thrown into a furnace fire
Shadrach, Meshach, and Abednego
Refused to do a such thing
But how dare they defy
The great and powerful Babylonian King
The king could not believe
These three Jews would not obey
The angry king told the three of them
You should certainly do as I say
The three men said of themselves
They would not defend
God was on their side
This situation He would amend
Even if God did not intervene
They said they would be okay
They knew their God had power, regardless
To step in and save the day

The three would not offend their True God
By worshipping an idol god
The prideful king was humiliated
He ordered for them to be tied
They were thrown into the fiery furnace
Which was heated seven times more
But upon taking another look
There was an extra man walking the furnace floor
Weren't there three
Three we threw into the fire?
Yes, certainly, there was three
Your Majesty, Royal Sire
Instead of a troubled trio
I see a peaceful quad
And the mysterious fourth man
He looks like the Son of God
What has happened here?
I have not seen this in all my days
Please come out of there
Your God deserves all the nations' praise
Everyone should show respect
To their God to whom they're devoted
Because of their faith in God
The three were all promoted

Food for Thought, Heart, and Spirit:

- Some leaders may forget about God, but we must always remember our God and remain faithful.

- God's people cannot dishonor Him to please others, fit in, nor to meet someone else's agenda.
- When you stand your ground in Godly living, others may become offended.
- While serving God, His people may be put in uncomfortable or even scary situations.
- God will deliver us one way or another.
- Beware to those who harm God's people, even at another's command.
- Our obedience to God and even the results of our obedience to God can serve as a testimony to others about God's goodness, mercy, and faithfulness.
- Our lives should help others to see our Almighty God and learn of Him.
- God gives promotions – God's people are promoted through obedience and faithfulness to Him.

KING NEBUCHADNEZZAR IS HUMBLED BY GOD

I, Nebuchadnezzar, want to tell of the
Signs and wonders God performed for me
I had a peculiar dream
About a strong and humongous tree
I was quite afraid
I was even terrified
Daniel's God can reveal all things
So his presence I required
Daniel, here's my dream
Please interpret this dream for me
There's no dream or mystery
Whose meaning you cannot see
In the dream, there was an enormous tree
Its top touched the sky
Visible to the ends of the earth
By each and every eye
The leaves were quite beautiful
The fruit was aplenty
The tree provided the animals shelter
This flourishing tree fed many
I looked and I saw a Holy messenger
Had come down before me
He called in a very loud voice,
Cut down that tree
Trim off its branches, cut off its leaves,
Scatter its lustrous fruit
But bound with iron and bronze
Remained the stump and the root

In the rain with the plants and animals
Is where this man shall live
From the mind of a man
To that of an animal, the Holy One will give
From that of a man to that of an animal
Shall describe his weary mind
Until time passes
Passes seven times
The Holy One declared the verdict
The messenger announced the decision
Daniel, I'm trusting you
To give me an explanation with precision

Daniel was also puzzled
He too was afraid
The king tried to reassure Daniel
Told him not to be dismayed
Daniel told the king,
If only it wasn't about you
It is you who will eat with animals
Be soaked by heaven's dew
Quickly renounce your sins
By doing what is right
For your wayward wickedness
Your soul must feel contrite
When you admit that the Almighty One
Is always in control
You will be restored to the throne
Please listen to what you've been told

The dream was not fulfilled
Until a whole year had gone by
When the king decided to announce,
"What a great king am I!"
Even as he spoke these words
Of pompous pride from his roof
God spoke back to him
With words of reproof
Your royal authority has been taken
Although you'd already been warned
You did not care to listen
Your nightmare is about to be born
Seven times will pass
Before you will come to your senses
Acknowledge God of all kingdoms
Who gives them to whom he wishes
The dream was fulfilled
No, not later, but right now
The king, King Nebuchadnezzar
He ate grass like a cow
His hair grew like the feathers of an eagle
His nails like that of a bird
Turned to God after seven times passed
Was restored and praised God till all had heard
The king resolved that right and just indeed
Describes this Amazing Almighty God
Able to reach and humble all
Who walks in ungodly pride

Food for Thought, Heart, and Spirit:

- Tell others about God's goodness, God's mercy, and His power.
- God knows how to get our attention.
- God's people must maintain open communication with Him not only for ourselves, but because others will depend on us to help them understand God's move on their lives.
- Being a messenger for God is not always easy nor comfortable, but we must deliver God's truth.
- In addition to the message of God's mercy, God's people must be willing to share the message of God's consequences for disobedience. There are sure and certain chastisements for not acknowledging and yielding to the Almighty God.
- We can avoid the sure justice of God against us if we turn from sin, reject sin, and do what is right.
- God's judgement and punishment is not always meant to "kill." Oftentimes, God's judgement and chastisement provide us with another opportunity to accept God.
- Like every good father, chastisement is a show of love.
- It is not God's will that we die in sin. God wants us to turn to Him, worship Him, and love Him. He already loves us.
- We have an opportunity to receive God as the authority in our lives before judgement and before we lose years of our lives.

KING BELSHAZZAR'S REIGN IS TERMINATED BY GOD

King Belshazzar hosted a private party
He wanted to impress his guests
They drank wine and ate royal food
But he wanted more finesse
He asked for the golden goblets
Taken from Jerusalem's holy temple
Determined to show off but soon found out
It wasn't quite that simple
His nobles, their wives, and concubines
Drank wine from the silver and gold
They even praised idol gods as though
The story of his father was never told
Suddenly the fingers of a human hand
Appeared and wrote on the wall
The king got so pale and weak
His knees so shook to nearly fall
The king summoned his advisors
To tell him what the writing means
Whoever can explain the writing
Will be third to the king
But none of the king's advisors could read
The writing nor tell what it meant
The king stood shaking, terrified
His nerves were completely spent
The queen heard the commotion
She went to see what was the trouble

She told the kind not to worry
There's a man of God who is noble
Your father, King Nebuchadnezzar
Appointed him as the advisors' chief
His intelligence and Godly wisdom
No other man can beat
Daniel was taken to the king
Promised royal gifts of the land
You can have these things
If you can tell the writing of the hand
Daniel said, keep your gifts
But I'll tell you what the writing means
I went through the same thing
With the last prideful king
King Nebuchadnezzar had power
To do things his own way
But God humbled him
Then He turned from his wicked ways
But you, Belshazzar, his son,
Did not learn though you knew this all
The writing says that you
From your kingdom are about to fall
God has numbered the days of your reign
Brought them to an end
There is nothing you can do
Not me, your mom, nor friend
You have been weighed in the scales
You have been found wanting
You knew you were doing wrong
Foolishly you changed nothing
So your kingdom is divided
Given to the Persians and the Medes

The Babylonian king died that very night
He didn't live another week

Food for Thought, Heart, and Spirit:

- God is able to humble those who refuse to humble themselves.
- A person's very life and soul are at risk when one knowingly takes something that has been dedicated to God and misuses it.
- God speaks to us regularly. We must be willing to listen. It is quite a gamble to push God to anger before we want to know what He is saying to us.
- It is not God's will that we must all learn through the sufferings of our own sin. God teaches us how to live both regarding what to do and what not to do through the examples of others.
- God loves us and wants to restore us to Him through repentance.
- In order to serve God, we must humble ourselves by honoring God as the ruler of our lives and our moral compass. God's opinion must be first priority in our decision making.
- To reject God is to welcome death and destruction.

DANIEL SURVIVED THE LION'S DEN

Always a man of God
Daniel found favor with another king
King Darius made Daniel an admin
One with superior ranking
About to become promoted
All the way to the top
The jealous men under him decided
This they would have to stop
But Daniel is an honest man they admitted
Nothing wrong that we can see
Except he loves his God
So we need a religious decree

The group of men went to the king
With their preplanned manipulative praise
You should have everyone
Worship only you for thirty days
If anyone breaks the law
That you yourself have penned
They shall be immediately thrown
Directly into the lion's den
Put it in writing so it cannot be altered
Neither can it be repealed
The king did so but not knowing
It was his best man they were trying to kill
Danial prayed to God
Just as he had done before
Opened his windows to Jerusalem
Put his knees to the floor

The group found Daniel praying
As they figured one later day
They went back to the king and reminded him
Of the decree that he had made
Kind Darius said yes, the word I gave
It's active and stands still
The group said, It's Daniel,
He does not abide by your will
He still worships his God
Each and every day
The king was not sure
Of what he should even say
Kind Darius wanted to save this
Godly humble man
But he had been tricked by pride
Into the envious, jealous men's plan
Into the vicious lion's den
Daniel, they spitefully threw
The sorrowful king said to him,
I hope your God saves you

A stone was brought and placed
Over the mouth of the lion's den
The king was disturbed but
His word he could not bend
The king went back to his palace
He certainly could not eat
He did not want to be entertained
Nor could he even sleep

The anxious king jumped up
At the sky's first morning light
He had to know if Daniel
Had survived the dangerous night
King Darius anxiously hurried
For he wished he already knew
Daniel, he called out to him,
Was your God able to save you?

Daniel replied, God sent an angel
So yes, I am still here
He shut the mouth of the lion
No more need to fear
My God has protected me
I'm found innocent in His sight
Nor have I ever wronged you
By you I've only done right

Marks, wounds, nor injury
On Daniel none were found
Because his trust in God
Remained always sound
The king gave the order
Daniel was lifted from the lion's den
Then the king ordered the group of men
To be thrown into the lion's pen
Not only the men, but include
Their wives and their kids
Before they touched the bottom,
They were torn into bits
King Darius wrote to the nations
His kingdom, every part

You must fear, honor, and reverence
Daniel's God in your heart

He rescues and he saves
For He is the living God
He performs signs and wonders in the heaven's
And on earth, for He is the living God
His kingdom will never be destroyed
For He is the living God
His dominion will never end
For He is the living God

Daniel continued to prosper
His unshaken faith remained
Throughout both King Darius and
Cyrus the Persian's royal reign

Food for Thought, Heart, and Spirit:

- God's people will be known for and promoted through Godly character.
- There are some people who will allow the devil to use them to target God's people for harm.
- Those who target God's people will order their own death, their own destruction, and their own downfall.
- We serve a living God who will be faithful to us if we will be faithful to Him.

Part II:

Karma is Never a Coincidence

Based on the Biblical book of Esther:
Chapters 1-10

7 Do not be deceived: God cannot be
mocked. A man reaps what he
sows. 8 Whoever sows to please their
flesh, from the flesh will reap
destruction; whoever sows to please the
Spirit, from the Spirit will reap eternal
life. 9 Let us not become weary in doing
good, for at the proper time we will reap
a harvest if we do not give up.
Galatians 6:7-9 (NIV)

ROOM IS MADE FOR A NEW QUEEN

Now King Xerxes was the ruling king
From India all the way to Cush
He lived a luxurious life
A lavish life of plenty and much
A big beautiful banquet
He hosted during the reign of his third year
The Who's Who of everyone
Was expected to be there
Nobles and princes of the provinces
Were quite excited and certainly eager
The guest list included Persian military officials
All of the important leaders

The king wanted to impress his guests
He thought of so many ways
Xerxes displayed his wealth and glory
For a full one hundred and eighty days
He showed everyone the gold
The pearls and the sliver
White linen, costly stones
Purple material, marble pillars
At the end, there was a party
Everyone had plenty of wine

The king's wife, Vashti, and
The women partied at same time

King Xerxes was high in spirits

From the wine on the seventh day

He commanded Vashti to come to him
Put her beauty on display
His aids delivered the message
The queen refused to go
The king burned with anger
How dare she tell him no

He called his team of advisers
Who fully understood the times
They said he must do something
Concerned about their own wives
They will surely dishonor us
If she can dishonor you
Send her away to never again
Ever to approach you
Let this be known to all
Make it an official decree
Then find someone else to be queen
Who is more beautiful than she
When the other wives hear this
Then they will all know
To obey their own husbands and
Much respect they will show

Pleased with the advice
The king did what they proposed
Message delivered and received –
Let every man rule his household

Food for Thought, Heart, and Spirit:

- Arrogant pride has consequences.
- Be careful not to feed the need to show off.
- Pride can influence us to make bad decisions involving other people.
- Arrogant pride leads to embarrassment.
- Our decisions always affect those who are connected to us.

A NEW QUEEN

After his anger subsided
The king thought of his former wife
His personal assistants advised him
To move on with his life
Commissioners will gather young beautiful virgins
From all across your land
They will be placed in the care of Hegai
They'll be safe in his hands
The virgins will receive beauty treatments
They will look good to the eye
Then let the woman who pleases you best
Be made queen instead of Vashti

In the citadel of Susa
There was a Jewish man
A descendant from Jerusalem
Forced into a foreign land
Descendants from Jerusalem
Who had been taken to Babylon
Mordecai was the son of Jair,
Kish's great grandson
His cousin's name was Hadassah
Also known as Esther
Her features and form were lovely
One of the many virgins gathered together

Many girls were brought to Susa
Placed under Hegai's care

Esther found favor with him
Hagai took good care of her
He immediately provided beauty treatments
Along with special food
He assigned to her seven maids
Gave her the very best room

Neither Esther's nationality nor family
Was revealed to the rest
Mordecai had forbidden her
He knew it wouldn't stand the test
Mordecai worried for her
He paced outside the place
Keeping his ears wide open
Hoping to hear that she was safe

Before one could see the king
Twelve months of treatments came first
Six months of cosmetics and perfume
Six months of oil and myrrh
They could take whatever they wanted
From the harem where they lived
After their initial meeting with the king
They could only return when or if he so feel

When it was Esther's turn,
She would take only what Hegai suggest
As soon as the king saw her
He was attracted to her the best
He made her the newest queen
Placed a crown upon her head

Vashti's no longer the queen
Esther is queen instead
The king gave Esther a banquet
Invited the nobles and officials
He proclaimed a holiday for his new queen
Gave gifts and made it official

Queen Esther kept her background a secret
Mordecai continued to stay near
Sitting at the king's gate one day
He heard what he was supposed to hear
Two officers were angry that day
They plotted to kill the king
Mordecai told Queen Esther and
She turned the officers in
She was sure to give credit to Mordecai
It was the right thing to do
The officials were later executed
After the accusations were found to be true

Food for Thought, Heart, and Spirit:

- God is able to protect us and grant us favor with others regardless of the situation.
- God's presence in our lives makes His people stand out from the crowd.
- God will position us to be in the right place at the right time. In those moments, it is our responsibility to do the right thing.

HAMAN'S HURT PRIDE

King Xerxes honored Haman
Haman, the Agagite
A descendent against Israel
The Jews he did not like
The king honored Haman
Above all nobles was his position
The king ordered his respect
So Haman expected recognition
Royal officials at the king's gate
Knelt down to pay him respect
But no, not Mordecai,
No kneeling nor honor when they met

The royal officials asked of Mordecai
Why did he disobey
Mordecai ignored them however
No attention did he pay
They continued to speak to him
He continued to ignore
They decided to tell Haman
To see how he would abhor
To these men Mordecai told them
That he was a devoted and devout Jew
They wanted to see what Haman,
The Agagite, would do

When Haman saw that Mordecai
Did not kneel to pay respect

He not only wanted to kill Mordecai, but
Take all the Jews by their necks
In the twelfth year and twelfth month
of King Xerxes royal reign
Haman won the lot
He decided the next thing that came
Haman told the king
There were people of a separate group
They do not follow the king
Nor do what he said to do
He asked the king for permission
To take matters into his own hands
He even offered to pay the king
To do what he had planned
He said he would kill the people
Who were a part of this group
The king gave him permission –
Haman could do what he wanted to do
The king told him to keep his money
He gave him his signet ring
With this symbol of authority
Haman could do anything

The royal scribes were called
During the first month on the thirteenth day
Haman gave orders through letters
To ensure he would get his way
Written in the name of King Xerxes
Sealed with the signet ring
The king's lieutenants and governors
Were told to oversee this evil thing

The order was to kill
Each and every Jew
Men, women, and children
Both the old and the young too
This evil thing was to happen
All on a single day
The thirteenth day of the twelfth month of Adar –
This was to be that day
This message went out to all the people
Every province knew the plan
The city of Susa was mystified –
Now the targets of the land

Food for Thought, Heart, and Spirit:

- Godly obedience often proves to provide protection.
- God's people are instructed by God to worship Him alone.
- Beware and be aware of "Hamans."
- God's people live differently from others. Romans 12:2 explains that God's people do not conform to the ways of this sinful world.
- John 15:19 explains that God's people do not belong to the world, but have been chosen out of the world and because of this, the devil and people used by the devil will hate us.

FOR SUCH A TIME AS THIS

When Mordecai learned of Haman's
Vengeful vicious plans
He put on sackcloth and ashes
He was clearly a distressed man
Mordecai went to the king's gate
Where he resentfully cried out loud
He must stop this evil plan
He had to figure out how
The order of the king
Was delivered to all the Jews
Many lay in sackcloth and ashes
Distraught after getting the news

When Esther heard about Mordecai
She was concerned and upset
She sent out clothes for him
The clothes he would not accept
She sent out another aid
To find out what was wrong
Mordecai told him everything
About the trouble for all at home
Mordecai sent back to Esther
A copy of the vindictive order
He wanted her to plead with the king
To rescind the word of slaughter

The aid went back to Esther
Reported the problem taking Mordecai's breath

But to approach the king without his request
Is a reason to be put to death
He responded that she needed to do something
For her own life was at stake
He said that if she didn't
The Jews would be saved another way
And who knows, but that this is why
you are positioned in this place today

Esther told Mordecai that he and all the Jews
In Susa should go on a three-day fast
She and her attendants would do the same
She would act on this thing at last
I will go see the king
At the end of the three fasted days
Although it could cost me my very life
I will go to him anyway

Food for Thought, Heart, and Spirit:

- God puts His people in the right place at the right time to fulfil His purpose.
- God's people must be both obedient and prayerful in order to fulfil God's purpose.

FAVOR IN THE FACE OF HATRED

On the third day, Esther went to see the king
In her royal robe
Though her presence was not requested
He would be pleased with her she hoped
He was pleased indeed and welcomed her
To come closer, to come near
He told her that whatever she wished
He would grant and wanted to hear
She asked that he and Haman would come together
With her to dine
She did not reveal her request
Her request would come in due time
The king and Haman joined Esther
For a banquet later that same day
To the king's surprise, she did not reveal
What she was waiting to say
Instead, she requested that they
Would come together for another meal
This time on tomorrow
Her request she would surely reveal

When Haman left the banquet
He was feeling rather good
Until he saw Mordecai
Who wouldn't bow as Haman thought he should
Haman went home to his family
For an evening filled with brag
He bragged about his family, his wealth

About being the banquet stag
He went on to tell about the one thing
That frustrated and continued to bother
Mordecai still would not bow, kneel
Nor to him would he pay honor
Haman set up a seventy-five-foot pole
As advised by his friends and wife
The plan was to go to the king and request
This to be how Mordecai will die

Food for Thought, Heart, and Spirit:

- We must be in communication with God so He can guide us in what to do and what to say in certain situations.
- Arrogant pride enjoys having its ego stroked, but it is very fragile because it is based on temporary and compromising situations and relationships.
- Other ungodly people encouraged Haman's demonic hatred of Mordecai and the Jews. Why? Ephesians 6:12 explains that our struggle is not against flesh and blood, but against the rulers, against the authorities, against the powers of this dark world and against the spiritual forces of evil in the heavenly realms.

MORDECAI IS HONORED

The king could not sleep that night
So he decided to read a book
The book of his legal records
He decided to take a look
He was reminded of the time
When Mordecai reported the plot
The king wanted to know
How he had been thanked for his troth

Nothing has been done
Not yet for this man
The king wanted to reward him
Thank him for his stand
Haman had just arrived
To ask for Mordecai's death
The king asked for Haman's presence
They hadn't spoken yet
He asked, "What should I do
To honor an honorable man?"
Haman thought he would get
All that he can
He must be speaking of me
I am the man he upholds
I would give him a royal horse
Put on him a royal robe
I would slowly parade him
Through the city streets

Proclaiming his royal honor
For all of the people to see
Go do these things at once
You'll lead the horse, yes you
Do all that you have recommended
For Mordecai the Jew

Haman robed Mordecai
Led him through the city streets
Proclaiming his honor for all
For all the people to hear and see
Afterwards, Mordecai went back to rest
At the palace gate
Haman rushed home and told his wife
All about his day
She told him he must forget
About his malicious, murderous plan
Because now the Jew he hated
Was a famed and honored man
Haman was quite annoyed
For he knew what she said was true
How did the tables turn?
Now he must honor the Jew

It's time for Esther's banquet
Where the king wants to hear her voice
Haman had to hurry
To attend he had no choice

Food for Thought, Heart, and Spirit:

- Doing the right thing always pays off - even if not right away.
- Doing the “right thing” is living in obedience to God.

HAMAN EXECUTED

King Xerxes and Haman arrived to
Queen Esther's banquet to dine
Surely, you're going to tell me queen
What you have on your mind this time
The king encouraged Queen Esther
To share what she had to say
Whatever you request my lady
It will be granted this very day
Esther said to the king
Spare my people and spare my life
My people and I are set to be
Killed for unjust strife
If we were set to be slaves
I would not have complained
But we are to be destroyed
Unjustly and viciously slain
Who is he?
Who would arrange such a plan?
It is this Haman
He is an evil man
The king jumped up and walked out
He walked out in a fit of rage
Haman knew to start counting
To start counting his very last days
Haman fell toward Esther
To beg for his life
The king came back and yelled,
"Get away from my wife!"

The king's aids were called in
They took Haman into their hold
There's a fifty-cubit pole set up
Near Haman's house they told
Haman had this pole
Put up for Mordecai the honored Jew
Haman
This pole shall be the death for you
Haman was indeed
Impaled on the seventy-five-foot pole
Only once it was done
The king's anger began to grow cold

Food for Thought, Heart, and Spirit:

- The devil never wins.
- "Hamans" never win.
- "Hamans" will always self-destruct.
- It is a person's choice to live for God or to live in opposition of God and relationally, in opposition of God's people.
- 2 Thessalonians 3:3 says, "But the Lord is faithful, and he will strengthen you and protect you from the evil one."
- God is able to protect us if we trust Him and allow Him to direct our actions, guide our decisions, and be the leader of our lives.

THE KING HELPS

That same day King Xerxes
Gave Queen Esther Haman's estate
Then Queen Esther told King Xerxes
How she and Mordecai relate
Taken away from Haman
Mordecai was given the signet ring
Esther gave to Mordecai
Haman's estate and everything
But Queen Esther found herself crying
Back at the feet of the king
Something must still be done about
The plan of my people's suffering
No previous document can be revoked
If sealed with the ring from me
So Queen Esther and Mordecai were given
Permission to write another decree
The month of Sivan, the third month
On the twenty-third day
Additional orders were written
Sent on their blessed way
They went to all 127 provinces
Stretching from India to Cush
Granting the Jews the right to protect themselves
Turn their enemies into mush
The month of Adar, the twelfth month
On the thirteenth day was the time
Every Jew would be ready and able
To protect their families from this crime

By the king's command, every province
Every citadel of Susa received the edict
The Jews celebration after this declaration
Was harmoniously grand, epic
The king had Mordecai clothed
In garments of blue and white
A purple robe and a large gold crown
He was certainly a welcomed sight
This was a time of celebration
Honor for all of the Jews
People even converted
Because of all they now knew

Food for Thought, Heart, and Spirit:

- God has an appointed time to reveal the hidden in each of us.
- What the devil means for our harm, God uses it to our benefit.
- Humility is honored by God.
- Being humble and remaining humble when put in positions of authority requires self-control.
- Self-control is a God-given strength.

CELEBRATION

The anticipated day finally came
To carry out the edict's plan
The enemy of the Jews
No longer had the upper hand
The Jews came together
To attack those who decided to hate
Once afraid, but afraid no more
Today, the enemy will pay
The enemy was afraid
All of the nobles were on Mordecai's side
Mordecai had become prominent
In the palace where honor reside

In the citadel of Susa,
The Jews killed five hundred men
As well as Haman's sons
Of which Haman and his wife had ten
The king later informed Esther
Of the results from earlier that day
Then asked her if there was anything more
Anything else she wanted to say
Esther said to extend the edict
Give the Jews in Susa another day
Impale Haman's ten sons
On poles to die the same way

Esther's request was indeed granted
What she asked was surely done

The next day in Susa, the Jews killed 300 men and
Impaled Haman's sons
In the provinces, the Jews killed
Seventy-five thousand more men
The next day, the celebrations started
Victory feasts began

Mordecai recorded it all
Sent letters near and far
Jews should celebrate annually
The fourteenth and fifteenth day of Adar
The Jews gratefully agreed
They planned amazing annual celebrations
For they had all been spared
Haman's planned annihilation
It was incredible to see the wicked plan
Haman had evilly devised
Is exactly the way Haman, his sons and
His soldiers died

Food for Thought, Heart, and Spirit:

- God's people are more than conquerors because God gives His people victory over evil.
- God will be sure to return to every man what he has prepared for others.

MORDECAI PROMOTED

King Xerxes promoted Mordecai
He became his second in command
Mordecai was highly respected
As a good and honorable man
He spoke up for his people
Not only for himself
Mordecai was greatly rewarded
With high authority and generous wealth

Food for Thought, Heart, and Spirit:

- God's people are strong, caring, bold in doing good, and respected among many.
- Obedience to God will cause some to hate you, but many to favor you even when they aren't sure why.
- John 10:10 ... But God comes so His people may have life and have an abundant life.

ABOUT THE AUTHOR

Esther Spells is the proud mother of an adult son and teenage daughter. She is also a proud educator who earned her BA and MA in education and serves as a public-school classroom teacher of English Language Arts. Teaching students for over twenty-five years and seeing them spiritually unprepared for life in this world has continued to feed a need to share the message of faith and hope. Esther's desire is to teach the message of the Bible through the genre of poetry. It would be one of her greatest life's accomplishments to help others internalize the hope, strength, and peace that comes with understanding God's Word.

www.ingramcontent.com/pod-product-compliance
Lightning Source LLC
LaVergne TN
LVHW050946080826
845145LV00004B/1431

* 9 7 8 0 5 7 8 8 3 9 8 2 0 *